the **Rat**

A guide to selection, housing, care,
nutrition, behaviour, health, breeding,
species and colours

Contents

the **Rat**

Foreword

Whenever you're planning to buy a pet, it's important to get plenty of information well in advance, even if your preference is for a small animal like a rat.
Is the animal right for your family? How much work is associated with caring for it, and how much will that cost? Can you cuddle it or only view it from a safe distance? This book will give you an overview over the origins of rats and mice, feeding, care, reproduction and the most common ailments and problems with rats. It is also intended to be a guideline for responsible buying and keeping of rats.

A separate chapter is devoted to special rats. These are rats that are possibly related to the tame rat and some varieties kept as pets by experienced enthusiasts.

About Pets

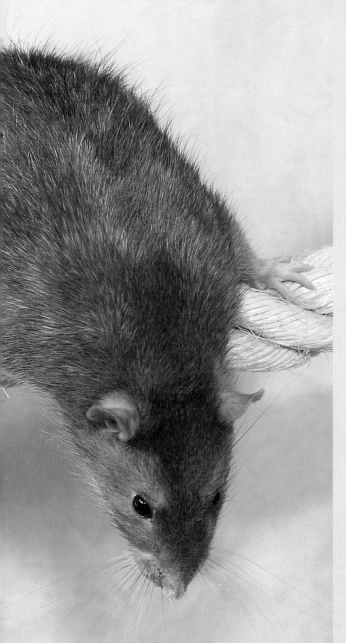

about pets

A Publication of About Pets.

ISBN 1852792183
First printing: September 2003
Second printing: June 2005
Third revised printing 2007

Original title: de tamme rat
© 1998 - 2007 Welzo Media Productions bv,
About Pets,
Warffum, the Netherlands
http://www.aboutpets.info

Photos:
Rob Doolaard, Rob Dekker and
Anneke Vermeulen-Slik

Printed in China

When we talk about rats, most people prefer to change the subject. We have mixed feelings about rats and plenty of prejudices.

However, there are enormous differences between wild rats and the fancy rat. We would prefer not to meet up with wild rats; they live in sewers, smell, are aggressive and spread serious diseases (in the past the bubonic plague). But their tame counterparts are the complete opposite, they are loyal, affectionate and very cuddly.

The rat's place in the world
There are probably some thousand varieties of rats in the world. Even some that are called 'rats' are not real rats. Real rats belong to the order of the rodents (*Rodentia*). Rodents form the

largest group of mammals. Of all the mammals in the world, more than half are rodents. The order of rodents is divided into a number of sub-orders. Real rats belong to the sub-order of mice and rats (*Muridae*). This sub-order is then again divided into a number of genera. The real rat is a member of the *Rattus genus*. As we mentioned, not all 'rats' are actually rats. The Desert Rat and the Beaver Rat belong to other sub-orders and genera and we will not cover those in this book.

The rat and the mouse
The rat and the mouse are closely related because they belong to the same sub-order. In zoological terms they are the same. Mice and rats have the same form, similar behaviour and identical reproduction. The only significant

difference is their size. Rats are bigger than mice. Within the sub-order of mice and rats, any animal smaller than thirteen to fifteen centimetres is a mouse, and anything larger is a rat. The *Muridae* sub-order includes some 1500 different (sub)varieties. The smallest is the African Dwarf Mouse, which only grows to five centimetres. The Giant Bark Rat is the largest at fifty centimetres. The rats that we know could almost be called civilised, as they live near humans, unlike most other rat varieties.

Rats can generally adapt to their environment extremely well. Many varieties actually live in trees, for example, even though they're not specifically built for that.

The Brown and the Black Rat
To understand the nature of the fancy rat, we need to look at two of their 'wild' counterparts: the Brown and the Black Rat.

The Brown Rat (*Rattus norvegicus*), despite being a sewer rat, is the ancestor of our rats. It lives in sewers, houses, barns, on refuse tips and countless other places. Whether in a tropical jungle or a big city, the Brown Rat feels at home anywhere.

The Black Rat (*Rattus rattus*), also known as the 'Roof Rat', is more slender and darker in colour than its brown brothers and sisters. It is also much less common.

Black Rats prefer to live in houses, where they go for high, dry roofs and attics. Brown Rats prefer cool, damp cellars and spaces under the house. The Black Rat is rarely found in Europe.

Distribution
The Brown Rat originates in Northern China and Mongolia. After the domestic mouse, it's one of the most common mammals in the world. There is practically no country where the Brown Rat is not found.

The reason for this worldwide distribution is in fact man's urge to

Brown Rat

travel. At the time man began to investigate what was beyond the horizon, rats went with him. These rats boarded ships together with humans; here they found damp dark hideaways and food. Rats are excellent swimmers and climbers, and got onto ships by climbing their anchor chains. Thus they spread over the whole world, first arriving in ports and then spreading inland in crates and barrels transported along dirt roads, and later by train.

One story is that large numbers crossed the river Volga in Russia in 1727 and thus got to Europe, although Brown Rats were found in Central Europe around the year 1500.

The Black Rat was found in Western Europe during the ice age and this is probably its origin. Two thousand years ago, Black Rats were found in the Mediterranean countries. The Black Rat also travelled by ship. They are real 'mariners': 95 percent of rats that live on ships are Black Rats.

Domestication

The fancy rat nowadays kept as a pet has descended from the Brown Rat. Indeed their appearance is similar, but their behaviour has changed considerably. Scientists began to keep Brown Rats as experimental animals early in the nineteenth century. In the

beginning, they studied these animals' build and behaviour. Later, medical experiments were also carried out on rats for the development of new medicines and treatment methods. A large group of rats not used as test subject were kept as 'breeding stock', while a number of their young were used for experiments.

Slowly, these laboratory rats became less and less wild and, over time, actually became tame. These are the true ancestors of our fancy rat.

Black Rat

Brown Rats live all over the world in widely differing conditions: as pets, but also as ship rats, sewer rats and farm rats, in the cold North or the hot South, and in all possible situations. This shows how adaptable they are to their environment.

Intelligence

The rat's ability to adapt arises from its high level of intelligence. A rat is a master at thinking out solutions for complicated problems.

A hard, round duck's egg is a tasty snack, but how does one eat it? A rat will roll the egg with its front paws to an edge and then throw it over. There's food to be found on the surface of the water, but how do you get to it? A rat will climb onto a floating plant and drift downstream. There are countless examples of the rat's inventiveness. Rats are exceptionally easy to train and you can teach them all kinds of tricks. They can find their way through a maze, run through an obstacle course or through a slalom; with a little training, it's no problem.

Gregarious animals

A rat is a gregarious animal by nature and is much more content living in small or large groups. A fancy rat can be kept alone but it then needs a lot more attention from its owner, so it's preferable to keep at least two rats together.

Taming

Rats are curious animals by nature. Kept as a pet, a fancy rat will almost never be aggressive, but

you must give it regular attention and take it out of its cage from time to time. If you don't, the animal will gradually become shy and in the end will seldom appear. If you hold a rat in your hands regularly from an age of five or six weeks, give it a treat now and then and let it run around on your lap, you will soon have a loyal comrade.

A rat on your shoulder

A rat will happily sit on your shoulder, but it has to be taught to do this. It will enjoy such a high observation post, but will also enjoy sniffing around. If you want to walk around with your rat on your shoulder, you have to teach the animal to sit still. When you put a young rat on your shoulder, it will to walk around curiously. Put it back in place if it decides to leave your shoulder. It can take hours and lots of patience, but there will certainly come a moment when the animal will sit still. Teach your rat that it can only get off your shoulder when there's a hand close by that it can step onto. A young animal may leave some droppings or urine on your shoulder but this generally stops once it's a little older.

Rats and other animals

In many cases, rats get on well with other pets, however care should be taken. Cats, dogs and ferrets will view a rat, especially a young one, as a tasty snack.

Most dogs can get used to being with a rat if you supervise the process closely. Always be present and watch out, especially with smaller hunting dogs such as terriers that may still be crazy about rats. Adult rats usually get on well with cats, but rats can never be kept with hamsters, mice, gerbils or birds. The chances are the rat will view these as an extra on its menu. Guinea pigs and rabbits are afraid of rats by nature and will feel threatened.

**A fancy rat is easy to keep. It doesn't have special dietary needs, is happy with a simple home and needs no special care.
But never buy a pet on impulse, not even a rat.**

Remember that a pet is totally dependent on you. It needs food and drink every day, its cage needs cleaning and it has a right to some attention. Get as much information as you need in advance before deciding whether to buy a fancy rat. A lot of animal suffering is the result of ignorance or of disappointment following a poorly considered buy.

Remember that not everyone likes rats, so discuss it with your family or housemates, who should approve. It's no fun having an ani-

mal in the house that makes a housemate's flesh creep! Sometimes, a churlish teenager may buy a rat to show off and train, and perhaps to annoy his parents a little. Once the fun wears off, the poor rat is left fend for itself. Perhaps it's superfluous, but a pet is no toy that you can put away when you've finished with it. All in all, a pet kept responsibly usually brings lots of pleasure; it's like having a piece of nature in the house, and a rat is nice, affectionate and devoted. It's also an excellent pet for children, as it's quiet and can stand the odd knock or two. A rat will only ever bite when it feels very threatened.

One or more
There are various ways to keep rats: one on its own, a pair or a whole group. Each method has its

Purchase

the **Rat**

own requirements. However it's important to remember that rats are gregarious animals that always need company. It's cruel to keep a rat alone in a cage with no attention. The animal will become shy, and possibly aggressive, so if you plan to keep a rat on its own, you must give it attention every day. A pair of males or two females is the simplest way to keep rats. They have their own company, but still get attached to their keeper(s).

Rats that live in larger groups (more than eight animals) will hardly get attached to humans. If you plan to keep a larger group, it's not a good idea to keep males and females together. You won't be able to see who is mating with whom and in-breeding may be the result; the females will also be constantly pregnant, which is bad for their health.

Before buying a group of rats, think about what you want to do with them. If you want to mate them it's best to keep them in pairs or smaller groups, males and females separately. When you want to breed a litter, you can put a male and a female together. Then you will know which is the father of the young, and how many litters the mother has borne.

If you want to keep a small group of fancy rats, but not get ship loads of young, then choose a group of males or females.

Where to buy

The best place to buy a fancy rat is from a rat lover that breeds the occasional litter. These animals have usually been lovingly cared for. The young are not separated from their mother too early, and the mother will not have borne too many litters. But finding such a fancy rat lover may be difficult. Rat lovers often take young rats to a pet shop, where you might also buy them. Be sure it's a good pet shop where the animals are properly kept in hygienic conditions, and where you get plenty of good advice.

Exhibitions and animal shows can also be good opportunities to buy

Getting your rat home

You've bought your rat and now you've got to get it home. Sellers often pack rodents into so-called bird cartons. These are small cardboard boxes designed to transport birds. But birds don't gnaw, rats do. Sometimes this will work and the young rat is too overawed to gnaw. But it's often a race against the clock: will the rat succeed in gnawing its way out before the end of the journey?

A better method is to transport your rat in a transport cage or tray. This may be more expensive than a cardboard box, but it can be used again if you're taking your rat on a trip, or need to clean its cage. Remember that your rat will grow, so make sure your cage is big enough. Never leave your rat in a cage in a car standing in the sun. The high temperature that develops there can be fatal for the animal.

Things to watch out for

If you're planning to buy a fancy rat, watch out for the following points:

- The animal must be healthy. A healthy rat has bright eyes and is lively. Sexual organs must be clean. Its coat should be glossy and free of scabs or wounds.
- Look especially for lumps or swellings. Some strains are very vulnerable to cancerous tumours and abscesses.

a fancy rat. These are usually held in the autumn and winter all over the country. Read more about these in the chapter 'Shows'. Animals sold here by breeders usually don't meet the high demands placed on them by show judges. They will be healthy and strong, but may not quite be the right colour, for instance. A (animal) market or flea market is certainly not the right place to buy a pet! If you want to buy a pet, think about it carefully and don't buy on impulse during your holiday or on a day out. Many examples of animal cruelty can be seen at animal markets. These traders breed animals to make a lot of money fast, and will continue doing so as long as they can sell their animals.

You may detect swellings in arm-pits, the groin and around its teats.

- Its eyes should be dry. Wet eyes are a sign of a cold, usually caused by draughts. Sneezing and sniffing are also a sign of a cold or pneumonia.
- Teeth and nails should not be too long.
- The animal should not be too young. Rats are sometimes offered for sale at three or four weeks old with the argument that they can be tamed quickly and are no longer taking their mother's milk. This is rubbish: a rat of five or six weeks will be just as tame, and has benefited from the sense of security of being with its mother.
- However, your rat should not be too old. Older animals die sooner of course, but also find it more difficult to adapt to new surroundings. You can recognise older animals by their coat, which is thicker and tougher than on younger animals. Older males often have a yellowish belly.
- Look closely at the other animals in its cage. If they look sick or weak there's a good chance that your new acquisition is also unhealthy.
- Watch out for unusual movements. Some rats swing their body or head. This can be the result of a brain disorder due to in-breeding. With rats with light eye colours, these movements are regarded as normal.

- A rat should be long, slim and sturdy, not too thin, but not too fat either. A slender female with a fat belly is pregnant.
- Never buy a female that is being sold from a mixed group with rats of different ages.
  You wouldn't be the first to be surprised with a litter of young after a few weeks. Sometimes a rat can be fertile at an age of six weeks.

Feeding

Day-in, day-out for years on end, rodents are fed the same thing: mixed rodent food. This consists of mixed grain with oats, maize, sunflower seeds, rye and pressed grass pellets.

However, research into the feeding habits of rodents in the wild has shown that they generally need a quite different and more varied diet.

Feeding in the wild
Rats in the wild will eat practically anything and are not at all fussy. They eat plant parts such as seeds, corn, fruit and young shoots, but prefer animal foods. Small insects and mammals, eggs and carrion are regular items on the menu.
Rats are good swimmers and excellent fishermen.

Feeding in captivity
Rats (and other rodents) are able to survive for long periods in difficult conditions because of their tremendous capacity to adapt. Years of eating the same one-sided rodent food won't kill them, but it seems illogical to feed rodents that need a varied diet the same thing all the time. Rodent breeders understand that and mix their animals' food themselves.

When you consider their feeding habits in the wild, it seems unlikely that a rat will thrive on a diet consisting only of vegetable ingredients. "Old-fashioned" foods contained almost no animal content and thus hardly any proteins. Fortunately a lot has changed in this field over the last few years. Major manufacturers have developed special foods for each variety

of small rodent. So there are very good foods available for the rat, but take care that they contain animal proteins. Whenever you buy any other food, take care that its structure is not too coarse. Rabbit food is certainly not suitable, nor are grass pellets (in the form of little dark green sticks). If you do use mixed rodent food, you can supplement it with cat or dog biscuits.

Whatever food you buy, look out for the date of manufacture. Food that is older than three months loses a lot of its goodness. Never buy too much food at once.

Just like humans, animals also like variety, but never give rodents sweets, crisps, biscuits or sugar lumps. The salt and sugar these foods contain can make them seriously ill. If you want to give your rat a treat once in a while, there are plenty of healthy pet snacks that you can use to put something special on the menu.

Pressed pellets
Pet shops also stock ready-made foods in the form of pressed pellets. These pellets all look the same and have the same ingredients. Many breeders and laboratories give their animals such

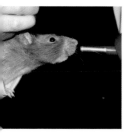

foods, because then they're sure that each animal gets all the nutrition it needs. Apart from that, a lot less food is wasted as the animals don't pick out what they like best, leaving the rest. But the question is whether they really like getting the same food every day.

Vegetables

Rats enjoy most sorts of vegetables. Because, like humans, they each have their personal likes and dislikes, try different vegetables to find out what your rat likes best. Don't feed it too much lettuce or cabbage as these may cause intestinal problems,

Sweets can cause serious digestion problems

Fruit

Most rodents, including rats, enjoy fruit. What sort is their favourite depends on the animal. Almost every rodent loves apple, pear, peach, raspberries, melon, berries and banana. Most animals find citrus fruits such as oranges and mandarines too sour, but some seem to enjoy them. Just like vegetables, too much of a good thing can be harmful. Take care to remove any pieces of fruit or vegetables from the cage that have not been eaten at once. There is a chance they will start to rot, which could make your rat ill.

Eating droppings

Almost all rodents eat their own droppings from time to time. This is not only normal, but also necessary. During the digestion process, vitamin B12 is produced in the intestines. By eating their droppings the animals take in this important vitamin.

Young rats eat their parents' droppings, because they contain the bacteria they need to be able to create vitamin B12 in their own intestines during digestion.

Vitamins and minerals

Vitamins and minerals are elements every living being needs to stay healthy. As long as a rat enjoys a good, varied diet it does not need additional vitamins and minerals. These are in its food. The chapter "*Health*" contains

the **Rat**

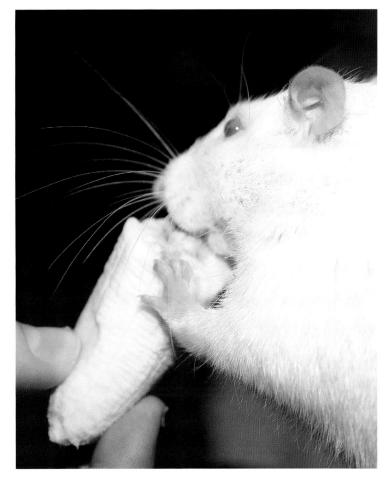

Water bottle

Mineral lick

Rodent snacks

more information about the consequences of an unbalanced diet.

Some breeders hang a so-called "mineral lick" in the cage. The animal takes in minerals by licking the stone and it seems that pregnant females, particularly, use them. You can also place small blocks of limestone in the cage. Your rat can gnaw on these and get extra calcium, while at the same time keeping its teeth sharp.

Water

In contrast to many other rodents, rats need a lot to drink and they must always have fresh water available, preferably in a drinking bottle. A dish of water is easily tipped over or fouled with shavings or other dirt.

Because rats can adapt to almost any environment, giving your rat a home will not be a problem. But there are a few rules you should observe. It's important that a rat feels safe and comfortable in its home.

It must not be too small or dangerous, and it should ensure the rat remails healthy.

The size of a cage depends on the amount of exercise your rat can get outside it. A rat frequently allowed to run free can live in a smaller cage than an animal which has to spend all its time in a cage. There are people that let their rat run free all the time, but even then it needs its own home that it can withdraw to and where it has its toilet.
A rat cage must be at least 60

centimetres long, 50 centimetres wide and 40 centimetres high. It's important that the rat can stand upright in it. A fancy rat that is rarely or never allowed to run free needs a considerably larger cage (80x50x40cm).

Types of cages
Because of their enormous ability to adapt, there are countless types of containers and cages that can be used to house a fancy rat. We'll look here at the pro's and con's of the most common types.

Wire cages
Rodents are often kept in wire cages. These consist of a plastic base with a top part of wire mesh. These cages are also suitable for rats as long as the space between the bars is not too wide. Rats can make

the **Rat**

themselves surprisingly thin and get through the bars.

A disadvantage of this type of cage is that the bars can rust over time, and the plastic base can be gnawed through. An advantage is that they offer good ventilation, but make sure it never stands in a draught. Rats love the horizontal bars in a wire cage as they can climb on them. Water bottles and other things can easily be mounted on the bars.

Another advantage of a wire cage is that it can easily be kept clean but, on the other hand, shavings or hay can easily be ejected when your fancy rat is playing or burrowing. Before buying such a cage check that it can easily be opened and closed and that there are no sharp parts, which could injure your rat.

Glass containers

An old aquarium or other type of glass container can also be used to house a rodent. These can be bought in a pet shop, but a used container can also be obtained cheaply. There are three types of glass container:

A solid glass container is made of one piece of glass. An advantage is that there are no sharp edges or corners where dirt can gather making it difficult to keep clean. A disadvantage is their weight, and if they're broken they can't be repaired and can only be thrown away.

The old-fashioned aquarium consists of a metal frame with panes of glass. Usually the glass is fixed to the frame with putty and the disadvantage here is that putty can dry out and crumble. A rat may easily eat this. Apart from that, panes may become loose or fall out. You can fix a "putty" container by taking it apart and refitting the panes with silicone sealant. Make sure there are no beads of silicone left which a rat may gnaw at.

Finally there's the frameless glass container. You can easily make

Wire cage

Glass container

dries. A disadvantage is that these containers often have sharp edges. You can smooth these down using fine sandpaper, or glue on plastic strips. You can easily put extra floors in the container by glueing glass or plastic supports to the walls and laying a glass plate on them. A glass container must have a lid. You can make one with a wooden frame and fine wire netting. Don't use a glass lid, as this offers no ventilation. Ventilation is both the strong point and the weak point of glass containers: the solid walls keep out draughts, but also most of the fresh air.

A glass container is usually easy to keep clean, the animals can easily be seen and there's no rubbish ejected. The disadvantage is that they can be very heavy and, being of glass, fragile.

this yourself with five panes of glass (one for the bottom and four for the sides). These panes are glued together with silicone sealant. Silicone takes a long time to dry so use masking tape to keep the container together while it

Plastic containers
There are various types of transparent plastic containers available, often called laboratory containers. These have a wire lid with an opening for the water bottle and a rack for food. Laboratories and breeders use these types of containers to keep animals as efficiently as possible.

However, these containers have several disadvantages: you can hardly see the animals, they can't stand upright in them, and their urine attacks the plastic.

Laboratory containers (like all transparent plastic containers) yellow with age and eventually become so scratched that they are opaque. If you keep animals for pleasure, don't put them in laboratory containers.

There are also so-called "Duna" cages, which consist of a coloured base and a transparent top. These cages are very roomy and high but have all the disadvantages of plastic containers and the ventilation is poor.

Wooden cages

If you're planning to use a wooden cage, remember that rats are rodents and they have absolutely no problem with wood. So make sure they can't get their teeth into any wood. Protecting corners and using smooth materials can prevent this. Another disadvantage is that wood absorbs moisture, and if urine gets into wood you'll never get it clean again. Waterproof the wood with non-toxic paint. Make sure no nails or spikes can become exposed should your rat manage to gnaw at the wood after all, as these can cause serious injury. Use wood plugs and glue.

In brief, the following points are most important for a good home for your rat: no sharp protuberances, no draughts, adequate ventilation, easy access, easy to keep clean and a high base (to prevent shavings being ejected).

The best place

The place where a cage stands is very important for the well-being of its resident(s). First you need to decide in which part of the house you want to keep your pet(s). Rats like company and enjoy being around humans, so the attic, garden shed or garage are unsuitable. The hallway (or other draughty place) is also unsuitable, as draughts must be prevented at all costs. Animals can often not deal with cooking steam, frying oil or butter, which counts the kitchen out, quite apart from the fact that many people would regard this as unhygienic.

A bedroom that is also used during the day may be a good alternative, but if it's only used for sleeping at night a rat will feel very lonely.

Plastic container

Caging

Wood shavings

Hay with herbs

Luxury bedding

The living room is actually the best room, but observe the following rules: a cage doesn't belong on the floor. It's draughty there and the cage can easily be kicked against, which will make your pet nervous. Put the cage on a low table or box. Rats love music but living permanently on top of a loud speaker or piano is too much of a good thing.

Daylight is important for most animals, but a rat should not sit in the full sun. The temperature (even in autumn or spring) can get so high that an animal can suffer heat-stroke, often with fatal consequences. A rat prefers a not too bright, but not too dark, corner. It doesn't like heat, so don't keep it too close to an open fire or radiator.

Cage litter

Sawdust or wood shavings are absolutely not suitable as litter in a rat's cage. Shavings contain too much dust, which rats are very sensitive to. Dust will slowly but surely get stuck in their bronchial tracts and can cause chronic breathing difficulties.

Good alternatives are shredded newspaper or paper (as long as the rats don't eat them). Beech shreddings, shredded straw or cat litter (not grit!) are also suitable.

Rats are particularly hygienic and will always use the same area as their toilet. A 'rat toilet', perhaps a

plastic container filled with cat litter, is a good idea. Use dust-free litter, with no sharp pieces, which is environmentally friendly and free of chemical additives (aromatics).

Interior

Rats love nesting material. You can use strips of cloth, paper or ready-made nesting material from a pet shop. Hay and straw contain too much dust and are often infested with mites. Rats enjoy pieces of cloth, but these will smell after a while and should be replaced or washed. Rats enjoy lying in a little hut. Plastic huts sold in shops are not really suitable; they are too small and your pets will chew them to destruction. A large glass jar (a pickle jar for example) is a good idea and is easily cleaned.

A flowerpot is also very suitable. Paint it to avoid urine absorption.

A rat's home should never be without a water bottle and food container. If possible hang the water bottle on the outside with the spout pointing in. The food container should not be too light, otherwise it is quickly overturned.

Finally, you can fit out your pet's home with climbing material. A branch, a parrot ladder, a piece of rope, some rocks or even old shoes are excellent toys and give the cage a pleasant look.

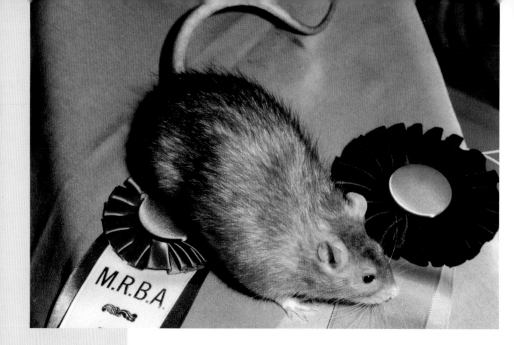

Many people breed rats as a hobby. Rat lovers have a number of containers with rats at home and try to breed beautiful examples with which they can win prizes.

During one-day shows, or even shows lasting several days, judges assess the animals that have been entered. The perfect rat must conform to the requirements set out in the Standard. If you're interested in taking up this hobby, you can contact the National Fancy Rat Society (see the chapter "*Addresses*").

Even if you're not planning to breed yourself but are interested in rodents, it's well worth the effort to visit a small animal show. You can get a lot of information and the breeders present often have good animals for sale.

The Standard

The standard describes how rats and other small rodents such as the Guinea Pig, the Hamster, the Mongolian Gerbil and the Mouse should ideally look. An animal entered for a competition can earn points in seven categories. In the score table you can see how many points a rat can score in each category. Points are deducted for any defects depending on their seriousness. The animal that finally scores the most points is the winner and earns the title 'best in show'.

Rats come in many more colours and markings than those included in the standard. But a colour or marking is only officially recognised if it's in the standard. For example: brown and cinnamon rats are described in the standard.

If a rat is entered that is not brown (like dark chocolate) and not cinnamon coloured, but a kind of medium brown, then it doesn't meet the requirements and will get a medium or poor score in the 'colour' category.

One can view the animal as a 'poor' brown or cinnamon rat. It is also possible to enter the animal as a 'new colour' for the standard, but not every mixture of two colours will automatically be approved. There are a number of requirements, which a colour or marking must meet to be included. At least four animals with the new colour or marking must be entered. There they are judged and possibly approved by the standard committee. The first step is preliminary recognition. If, after three years, there are enough animals with the new colour or marking, it is then fully recognised.

The judging

During a show, the animals entered are judged in the following categories:

Type and build

This part of the standard describes the fancy rat's form and build. A quote: "The body must be long and slender, curved at the loins so that the rump is finely arched. The animal must be strong and muscular, with a robust build. The tail is approximately twenty centimetres

Rex rat

Agouti

The judge

long. The tail runs flowingly from the hindquarters, is thick at the root and tapers gradually to a fine point. The front paws have four, and the rear paws five toes".

Size

A rat must be of considerable size. It should be approximately 24 centimetres long; an adult animal should weigh approximately 500 grams.

Coat and coat condition

The coat must be thick, smoothly laid-on and must not be too long or coarse. Tail, feet and ears are covered in thin fur. The coat must be slightly glossy.

Head and ears

Prize winner

The head is long, but the snout must not be too pointed. Eyes are large, ball-shaped and lively. Ears must be wide and blunt in form, not too large, slightly fleshy and set wide apart.

Topcoat and belly colour

Topcoat means the surface colour of the animal's back, the belly colour is the surface colour of the belly. The word 'surface' is of great importance here. A hair usually consists of various colours.

The base of a hair (at the skin) will be of a certain colour. The tip of the hair will be of the topcoat or belly colour. In some cases the middle part of the hair will also have yet another colour of its own. The topcoat and belly colours are important because the tips of the hair are obviously the most visible. The various topcoat and belly colours are what are described as colourings.

Middle and base colour

After reading the above, it's clear what is meant by middle and base colour. These colours become visible if you blow into the coat. The hair that lays back forms a rosette, clearly showing the middle and base colour.

Body condition and care

A rat must be sturdy and muscular. Its eyes are clear. A rat must not be thin, but also not fat. It should be made clear that rats sold in pet shops are not pedigree

rats. They have been bred as pets and not for showing. You could also call them 'medley rats', but they are often the nicest and best-natured animals.

But it's still a good idea to find out how much your companion conforms to the standard. Some categories, such as 'body condition and care' also count for a pet. So now and again, view your rat as if through a judge's eyes: is it not too thin or too fat? Is its coat properly cared for?

Colourings
The following colourings are recognised in the standard:

White Pink-Eyed: Everyone thinks that a white rat with pink eyes is an albino. But that's not always correct, because an albino possesses no pigment, while a white rat has a normal white colour. That's why this colouring is called 'White Pink-Eyed'.

White Dark-Eyed: This is a white rat with black or very dark-brown eyes.

Black: A perfect black rat is especially difficult to breed. The black must be as dark and even as possible. This colouring has nothing to do with the Black (Roof) Rat!

Brown: A brown rat should have the colour of black chocolate. This colouring was previously also cal-

led 'chocolate brown'. Judges prefer deep dark colours.

Champagne: A champagne-coloured rat is of a light crème to beige colour, with a reddish glow to its coat.

Crème: The colouring crème must be a soft cream colour.

Agouti: This is a spotted colouring, which also occurs in the wild. The spotting comes from the fact that its hairs have a black tip. In the hobby field this is called 'ticking' or 'wild colouring pattern'. The wild colouring of a rat has become fuller and deeper, with a red mahogany tint.

Show cages

Agouti

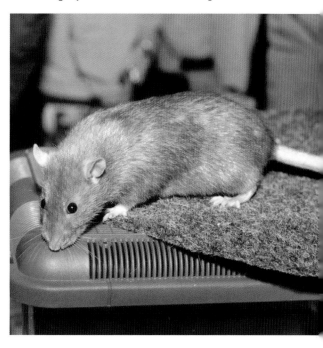

A broad 'saddle' stripe runs across its back.

Variegated: This is a spotted rat. The spots are approximately one centimetre in diameter.

Irish: Seen from above this is similar to a normal single-coloured rat, but a white triangle appears on its chest.

Siamese. The Siamese is actually not a marking but a livery. This rat is similar to a Siamese Cat. Its body is beige, its nose, ears and paws are dark:

Tailless rat

Hairless rat

Silvered: This is a warm yellowish colour. Silvering arises from transparent and white hair tips that make the coat appear more glossy.

Argente: This colouring is very similar to a darker silvered rat. However, the basic colour should be more bluish.

Cinnamon: This is the colour of cinnamon.

Markings

With rats a marking is understood to be a pattern of two colours, which is usually strictly laid down. The following markings are recognised in the standard:

Hooded: This is the most common marking. The rat's head is coloured (e.g. black, brown or crème) and its rear body is white.

Besides the above colourings there are a number of colours that are not yet recognised, but which occur frequently. Examples here are lilac, mink, blue, dove-grey, black silvered and birch. There are also some markings and liveries in so-called 'development': Capped, Masked, Newly-Hooded, Rus, Husky, Rex and Satin.

The breeding of rats over the years has not only led to splendid, healthy specimens but, alas, has also led to excesses. Such is the Dumbo (fortunately only in America), a rat with strikingly large ears. The Hairless is also very rare (also fortunately) in Europe. As the name suggests, the animal has almost no hair. The Tailless Rat is a mutation that has been deliberately bred in America and the UK. The Odd-Eyed has eyes of different colours.

Apart from the usual rats, a number of different rat species are sometimes kept as pets. Rat lovers and zoos are devoted to them, but not on a large scale and with varied success.

The Kowari

The Kowari (*Dasyurus byrney*), also known as Byrne's Marsupial Mouse or Brush-Tailed Rat is an excellent example of a rat that doesn't belong to the rat nor mouse family. It is an especially fascinating burrowing animal that is kept in captivity with mixed success (mostly in zoos). Only a few are kept in private households.

Its origin is in Central Australia where it lives alone or in small groups in desert areas. The Kowari is a nocturnal rover that feeds mostly on insects and lizards. It will also enjoy small birds or rodents. In the wild it reproduces in winter. After a pregnancy of 32 days, an average of five or six young are born. Kowaris can live to a high age.

The Fat Sand Rat

The Fat Sand Rat (*Psammomys obesus*) is not a real rat, but a gerbil. It is not suitable to be kept as a pet. A Fat Sand Rat fed on hamster food, for instance, will become very friendly, but will stop reproducing. If you give it just the right food (or other special green foods) it will reproduce, but also become particularly aggressive. The Fat Sand Rat is fifteen to eighteen centimetres long, with a tail of twelve to fifteen centimetres. It can store a reserve of fat under its skin and use this to survive periods where food is scarce.

The Gambian Pouched Rat

The Gambian Pouched Rat (*Cricetomys gambianus*) is a very special animal that has been kept as a pet by a few enthusiasts for a while. Scientists have long argued about whether this large animal (with a tail up to eighty centimetres long) belongs to the hamster family or the rat and mouse family. For the time being this animal is assigned a separate sub-family of the mouse and rat family.

The Gambian Pouched Rat is not suitable as a family pet. They withdraw to their burrow at the first sign of light and are not seen again. Direct sunlight can even kill them. The Gambian Pouched Rat can be viewed in the nocturnal animals sections of a few zoos.

The Nile Rat

The Nile (Grass) Rat (*Arvicanthis niloticus*) is indeed still kept as a pet, albeit on a moderate scale. This animal originates from the Nile Delta (Egypt) and other parts of the Arabian Peninsula. As its name suggests, it lives mostly in grasslands (savannahs). Grass Rats are undeniably group animals. In the wild their colonies can be up to a thousand animals. And in captivity too, they can only be kept in groups. They enjoy each other's company and during pregnancy the female can even remain in the group. A Grass Rat will typically bear two to six young.

Although Grass Rats can be kept as pets, they're not cuddly animals. They can be picked up without difficulty by their tail, but you can't set them on your hand, although they don't usually bite.

Gambian Pouched Rat

Special rats

Nile Rat

Black Rat

You can keep Grass Rats in a large glass aquarium (minimum 80 x 40 x 40 cm) with sawdust as litter and a large bundle of straw as nesting material. Although they like to get under the straw, they're not shy and will show themselves regularly. You can feed Grass Rats the same as normal rats.

The Black Rat

The Black Rat (*Rattus rattus*) as a species is not the same as a black coloured Brown Rat which we keep as a pet. This is a common mistake. A Black Rat is something of a variety between a domestic mouse and a (wild) Brown Rat. Its head is very pointed with relatively long whiskers and big eyes. The Black Rat is not always really black. Its topside is normally grey-brown to black and its belly is white to dark grey. Its coat also contains some longer hairs, which stand out clearly against a lighter background. Black Rats are far shyer than domestic rats and definitely not hand-tame. They can climb better than a Brown Rat, so they need a much larger cage (minimum 80 x 40 x 40 cm) with plenty of climbing and hideaway opportunities. Although many believe they own a real Black Rat, this is only seldom the case, because a real Black Rat is not a cuddly animal. You can keep them in groups and feed them with normal rat food. They also love the occasional mealworm or other insect.

There are other varieties of rats kept by rat lovers (and there will probably be more to come), such as the Cotton Rat (*Sigmodon hispides*), the Bamboo Rat (*Connomys badius*), the Short-tailed Hamster Rat, and the European Water Vole (*Arvicola terrestris*).

Because rats can adapt so well, they will usually survive in captivity. The following general rules apply to keeping special rat types:

- Rats live in colonies in the wild. Males and females live together.
- Rats are rodents, they have sharp teeth which will make short work of a wooden cage.

- Rats need a varied diet: seeds, grain, animal proteins, greens and fruit.
- Rats like twigs in their cage. They use them to gnaw on and for climbing.
- Special rat types need hide-aways. They feel more comfortable there and will show themselves more often. But don't use nesting boxes. Whenever a group of rats gets inside one of these, some animals may suffocate. Pieces of wood they can crawl under are better.

It is not advisable to start with an exotic variety if you have little experience with animals.

Black Rats

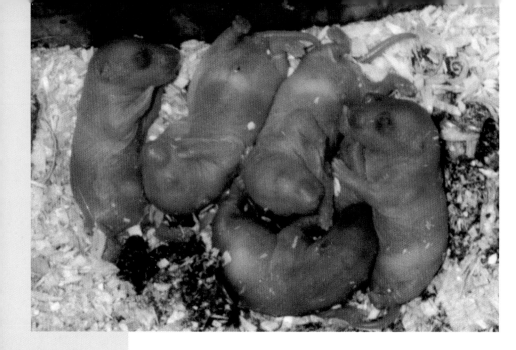

If you keep a male and a female rat together, there's a big chance you're going to get lots of baby rats in no time!. You need to carefully consider whether that is what you want.

A litter of young rats is nice, but after the second or third litter, it can be difficult to find good homes for the young. So think about reproduction (wanted or unwanted) before buying your pets.

Male or female
With rats the difference between the sexes can usually be seen at a glance by examining them under their tail.

As with most rodents, you can tell the sex of a rat from the space between its anus and its genital opening. This distance is much larger on males than on females. On grown males you can also see the scrotum. Unfortunately, inexperienced pet shop personnel often make mistakes when determining the sex of young animals. It can happen that two females suddenly seem to have young.

In-breeding
To breed responsibly, you must never put any male together with any female, because there is a high risk of in-breeding. For instance, if you've been given brother and sister from a neighbour's litter, it's better not to mate them. Pairing these animals together is a serious form of in-breeding, and who can guarantee that your neighbour's litter wasn't already the result of pairing brother and sister?

the **Rat**

Breeding

One instance of in-breeding is certainly not a disaster, but if it happens several times the results quickly become apparent. Young born from in-breeding get smaller and weaker each litter; the litters become smaller and smaller in number and, finally, young are born with in-born (lethal) defects.

Mating

If you keep a male and female together in a cage all the time, the young will arrive at random and unexpected times.

However, in most cases males and females live apart and they have to be brought together for mating to take place.

It's best to bring the female to the male. After all, he knows his own home well and won't have to check everything out before getting to work. For a successful pairing the female must be fertile and ready to mate, which happens every five days for a period of five or six hours. This period is called the 'oestrus', which you can recognise by the female's behaviour: if you tickle her back she will flap her ears and go into the mating position. However, this trick does not work with all females. If you can't tell the oestrus by this method, you'll have to risk an attempt five days in a row. A female that is not ready to mate will fight tooth and nail against an insistent male. If the female won't mate, but is happy to stay in the

vicinity of the male, leave them together for a week. Normally a successful mating will take place during that time.

During mating, the male will mount the female several times in a row. After a successful mating, the female will lose a drop of whitish slime within a day or so.

Pregnancy and birth

After a successful mating the fertilised egg nestles into the womb. A rat pregnancy lasts approximately 22 to 24 days and the female needs peace and quiet during this period. After a week or two she will become visibly thicker and must no longer be picked up. She now needs extra food and minerals. Give her a limestone block to lick and gnaw on. The female's instinct will tell her when she needs extra salts and minerals and she will get them by licking on the stone. You can also supplement the mother-to-be's diet with canned cat food.

Clean out the cage thoroughly a few days before the birth and put in extra nesting material. The birth itself is generally problem-free. The mother lays her young in the nest she prepared in advance. Very rarely an inexperienced mother may bear her young spread out all over the cage and then leave them to their fate. Pick up the young carefully with a cloth (or with textile gloves), lay them in the

nest and check that the mother takes care of them. Never pick up the young with your bare hands or with leather gloves. The mother will reject them because of the scent. After the birth the mother will eat the afterbirth. This is a relic of the wild. By eating the placenta she takes in extra nutrients. It also prevents animals or birds of prey smelling the afterbirth and attacking the young.

In most cases eight to ten young are born, sometimes even more. It is advisable to check whether there are any dead young animals in the nest. Do this carefully because the proud young mother can be aggressive against people or animals that threaten her young.

Development

After the first check, leave the nest in peace for a few days. Check after about four days if everything is in order. In most cases the young will be laying in the nest with full tummies. Sometimes there may be one underdeveloped

Reproduction of the rat

Sexual maturity:	from 56-60 days, sometimes from 30 days
Duration of fertile cycles:	6 days (per month)
Fertile for:	6 hours
Number of teats:	12
Separate parents at birth?	Yes, to prevent a new pregnancy
Length of pregnancy:	22-24 days
Number of litters per year:	3-6
Number of young:	4-16 (average 10, maximum 24)
Weight at birth:	approximately 5 grams
Female fertile after birth:	within 24 hours
Eyes open:	15-20 days
Suckling period:	28 days
Fertile months of female:	14, sometimes substantially more

baby, which is visibly smaller and thinner. Such an animal will often survive, but will remain smaller and puny. The first nest fur will be visible after a few days, and the animals open their eyes after about two weeks. Watch out for this, but the tots will certainly not open their eyes too early. The young will grow quickly. The nursing mother still needs extra food to keep the milk production going. After two weeks, the young have a short silky coat and markings and colour are clearly visible. The young rats now start to investigate the great wide world, but at first their mother will keep dragging them back to the nest. After a while she will give up and the young rats will play to their hearts' content climbing and scrambling all over the cage, so make sure they have enough toys and climbing opportunities.

The young now eat more and more. It's amazing how much food a nursing mother with growing offspring can process. After about four weeks, the young are practically self-sufficient.

The mother takes a young in her mouth to bring it to a safe place. She doesn't harm the young.

Rats are generally strong, lively animals that are seldom sick. If you look after your pets properly and give them the right food, you've much less chance of having a sick rat than someone who doesn't.

While you can't always avoid sicknesses, you can do a lot to reduce the risk.

Recognising sicknesses

A healthy rat is active and has bright eyes. When it wakes up, it immediately raises its snout to check out its surroundings. A sick rat will sit hunched up and retire to a quiet corner. If you notice that your rat has crept away for more than one day, and shows itself less often, then it's time to watch out for problems.

You can often recognise a sick rat by its eyes, anus, nose or breathing. Damp eyes, rattling, stuttering breathing or sneezing point to problems in the lungs or nasal passage. If its anus or belly is soiled, this is usually a sign of an intestinal condition.

Sick rats will eat less and irregularly. A shivering rat is running a fever. Often its coat will be dull and hairs stand upright. Put a sick rat in a warm, quiet place. If it won't drink, you can give it extra moist fruit such as pear or melon. Don't delay a visit to the vet's too long as some ailments can worsen rapidly.

Rats (and other rodents) have a red tear secretion around their eyes. This is caused by a colouring substance called porphyrine. This red colour is normal and clearly visible on light coloured rats. Excessive tears point to an ailment in the sinus cavity and are a cause for concern.

Digestion problems

Diarrhoea is one of the most common problems with rodents. It is usually caused by incorrect feeding or by food that has gone mouldy or bad. Vegetables contaminated with insecticides can also cause intestinal ailments (or worse). Feed a rat with intestinal problems boiled rice or rusk. If the problems are really serious, take it to the vet's quickly. A small animal suffering from serious diarrhoea can quickly become dehydrated.

The opposite problem is constipation. The animal can not empty its bowels, or only with difficulty. Its droppings are smaller and longer than normal and often very hard. The cause of constipation may be the wrong food, but possibly also a lack of exercise. Feed a rat suffering from constipation plum or peach and make sure it gets lots of exercise.

Overgrown teeth

Rodents and rabbits have teeth that grow continuously, and which wear themselves down by continuous gnawing. Normally, the teeth in the upper and lower jaws stand against each other restricting their growth, but if a tooth is in the wrong position because of an accident or due to a congenital deformation, it can just keep growing, even into the opposite jaw. This is called overgrown teeth. With such a long tooth, the animal can no longer eat and will eventually starve to death. If you notice that your rat is eating poorly or is dribbling at the mouth, you must check its teeth. If it has an overgrown tooth, the vet must clip it back. This will solve the problem but there's a big chance it will grow back. You can help prevent overgrown teeth by making sure there's enough material to gnaw at in the cage.

Deficiency ailments

An animal needs many different nutrients to live a healthy life. It must get these substances from its food. Some elements are necessary to keep it in proper condition. Calories are needed to keep its body at the right temperature. Vitamins, minerals and various other substances are indispensable to keep its body working properly. A rat that gets a well-balanced, varied diet will be sick less often than one that always gets one-sided food. A shortage of certain vitamins and minerals can cause diseases. The table on page 55 gives an overview of ailments caused by deficiencies.

Generally it makes no sense to give rats vitamin preparations. A proper diet provides everything the animal needs, but for a sick animal, extra vitamins may help it

Hairless rat

restore its strength. But use caution when giving such a preparation, because too much of a certain vitamin can also cause sicknesses!

Breathing problems

Incorrect housing is often the cause of diseases such as colds or pneumonia. Too often, rats get colds or pneumonia because their cage stands in a draught or their cage litter contains too much dust. A layman can not tell the difference between a heavy cold and pneumonia. Breathing is rattling and spluttering, its eyes are wet and the animal is apathetic. In the past, one assumed that this was caused by mycoplasma bacteria. However, research has shown that this bacteria is rarely the primary cause of the sickness. More usually, the cause is a chronic bronchitis caused by the Carr-bacillus. This slowly but surely drags the rat's condition down and makes it vulnerable to mycoplasma bacteria. It seems that rats exposed to ammoniac vapours and dust (a result of lack of hygiene and ventilation) are especially vulnerable to these ailments.

A rat with symptoms of a cold should be treated with antibiotics as quickly as possible.

Injuries

A rat can suffer injuries in various ways. They are normally social animals who feel comfortable in a group, so fighting injuries are seldom, except when too many rats are kept in too small a cage.

But an accident is more likely. A rat can fall and break or bruise something, get stuck in the door, be (literally) trampled underfoot etc.. So a rat can get injured in the normal course of life, but they are fortunately tough animals that can easily withstand the odd knock. External injuries heal quickly and only wounds with wide cuts need to be stitched. Keep any wounds clean, put your rat in a cage with paper as floor covering to avoid dust getting into the wound. Wounds frequently heal without being properly clean and an infection can then arise under the skin. The pus may cause an abscess,

Give your rat healthy food. Salty crackers are not healthy!

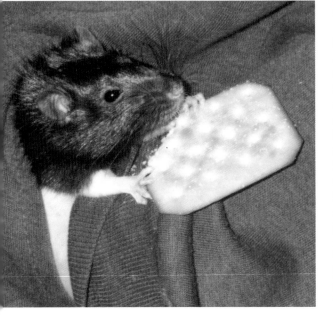

Deficiency of	Symptoms	Found in
Protein	Poor coat, hair loss, pneumonia, infertility and poor growth of young animals, aggression (both with too much and too little)	Peas, beans, soya, cheese
Vitamin A	Pneumonia, damage to mucous membrane or eyes, growth problems, diarrhoea and general infections, cramps, small litters	Root vegetables, egg-yolk, fresh greens, bananas and other fruit, cheese
Vitamin B complex	Hair loss, reduced fertility, weight loss, trembling, nervous symptoms, anaemia, infections	Oat flakes, greens, fruit, clover, dog biscuits, grains
Vitamin C	The rat produces this itself, deficiency rarely a problem Growth problems, poor bone condition	Greens, fruit
Vitamin D	Too much vitamin D causes calcium loss in bones and calcium deposits in blood vessels	Dairy products, egg-yolk
Vitamin E	Infertility, muscle infections, nervous problems, bleeding and poor growth of young animals	Egg-yolk, sprouting grains, fresh grains, greens
Vitamin K	(Nose) bleeding, poor healing of wounds and growth problems	Greens
Calcium	Normally produced in the animal's intestines. Lameness, calcium loss in bones and broken teeth	Mineral preparations, dairy products, sepia, varied diet
Potassium	Weight loss, heart problems and ascitis, wetness in open abdominal cavity	Fruit
Sodium	Can only occur with serious diarrhoea	Cheese, varied diet
Magnesium	Restlessness, irritability, cramps, diarrhoea and hair loss	Greens, grains
Iron	Anaemia, stomach and intestinal disorders, infertility	Greens, grains, meat
Iodine	Metabolic disorders and thyroid gland abnormalities	Greens, grains, water

Hairless rat

which can be very painful. Never open an abscess yourself, but take the animal to the vet's.

Rats can break bones too. If you notice a paw in an odd position, it may be broken. Plaster is not a solution for a rat. A splint is an option, but you should leave that to a vet. Incorrectly placed splints can cause the animal a lot of pain. Make sure it doesn't gnaw the splint to destruction because it will certainly try to. Patiently prevent it

from doing this for a few days until it accepts the splint.

If a rat gets stuck in a door or is trodden on, it may suffer internal injuries. The skin may be intact, but something may be damaged inside. Only a vet can help in this situation.

Skin conditions

Rats can suffer from various skin conditions. Many are caused by parasites; eczema, rashes, bald

spots and hair loss are regular occurrences with rats. Older males can have hormone problems causing skin conditions. The wrong food, too little exercise and mould can also lead to skin diseases. Rat pellagra is a disease causing abrasion and infections. This can result from a lack of vitamin B. If a rat that is fed properly and with a varied diet does get skin problems, a visit to the vet's is called for.

Tumours

One of the most common conditions suffered by (mostly older) rats and mice is a tumour. This is a swelling that may be benevolent or malignant (cancer). Males often suffer from tumours around the hips or groin (on the lymph glands), females are subject to tumours around the teats (breast cancer).

Vulnerability to tumours is largely genetic. Some strains suffer more than others. In-breeding also seems to play a role. There is some evidence that feeding pressed pellets (grass pellets) can cause tumours over time, due to various chemical additives (vitamins and medicines). A tumour can only be treated by a vet.

Parasites

Parasites are tiny organisms that live at the expense of their host. There are both internal and external parasites. Internal parasites (worms) live in the host's stomach and intestines. External parasites infest the skin or skin recesses (ears, hips and groin).

You can sometimes (but certainly not always) detect internal parasites by small white strings in your rat's droppings. The animal will slowly but surely become thin and

Flea

Mite

apathetic. Internal parasites can be treated with a worm cure, which your vet can prescribe.

External parasites such as fleas, lice, ticks and mites feed on blood or flaking skin. If you take care of good hygiene and look after your pets, you won't need to worry about parasites. A healthy rat has an acid skin that parasites don't like, but if its resistance is reduced a rat may become vulnerable. Alas, rats are often affected by burrowing mites, even when they're perfectly healthy. The burrowing mite is extremely infectious and is often spread at shows.

The condition must be treated with a series of injections.

Good medications against external parasites can be bought from your vet or pet shop. Always follow the instructions to the letter, as some parasites lay eggs that are not dealt with by these treatments. When these eggs hatch the pests are back, so you may have to keep repeating the treatment over a certain period.

Behaviour problems
Healthy animals, well looked after and from a strong strain, will typically not show behavioural pro-

the **Rat**

blems. Occasionally rats become compulsive washers, gnaw at cage bars for hours on end, show aggressive traits or run round in circles. These behaviour problems are often the result of boredom or in-breeding. Rats that are kept alone, or in too small a cage with a bare interior, display this kind of behaviour, and once it's started it's difficult to stop. Don't breed with animals that suffer from this kind of behaviour. Parents can pass on neurotic behaviour to their young.

Sunstroke

As we already mentioned, rats should never stand in the sun, even in spring or autumn. A glass container, especially, can quickly become an oven. A rat may be put outside in the sun but should always have some shade to withdraw to, but remember that a little hut in an overheated glass container won't offer any relief from the heat.

A rat with sunstroke will often lay flat on the ground huffing and puffing, its heart-rate and breathing are rapid. But the real harm can sometimes occur later: the rat simply collapses, becomes unconscious and has difficulty breathing. Put it in a quiet cool room as quickly as possible. You might want to wrap it in a wet towel. When it comes around, stop the cooling so that it can quietly get back to normal.

- Rats are real group animals. They are much happier living in a cage with other rats.
- Take rotting food out of the cage. It can cause disease.
- Take the time to visit a small animal or rat show.
- Rats must always have fresh water available.
- Never buy an animal too young.
- Never give vegetables in large quantities. Especially lettuce or cabbage can seriously affect the intestines.
- Give a rat opportunities to climb, clamber and play.
- Avoid in-breeding, not only with rats, but with all animals.
- Watch out for insecticides. If in doubt, wash fruit and vegetables thoroughly.
- Never buy a rat just to annoy others.

- Draughts, damp and incorrect feeding, cramped quarters and too many animals in too small a cage can all threaten your rat's health. Avoid them.
- Feed your rat special rat-food.
- Take care that food and water containers can't tip over.
- Isolate a patient with an infectious disease.
- Never keep your rats on shavings.
- You must find a good home for all your young rats.
- Rabbit food is not suitable for rats, because it contains ingredients that can affect the digestive system of small rodents.
- Never release a rat into the wild. It will not survive.
- Never transport a rat in a cardboard box. He might gnaw his way out.

Tips

the **Rat**

Becoming a member of a club can be very useful for good advice and interesting activities. Contact the club in case addresses or telephonenumbers have changed.

National Fancy Rat Society

The society's aims listed in its constitution are:

- To promote the propagation, study and exhibition of fancy rats.
- To publish the definition of the true type as the only recognised and unvarying standard by which fancy rats shall be judged, and to adopt standards relating to the various varieties.
- To urge the adoption of the standards of excellence upon breeders, judges and show committees as the only criteria of merit in breeding and awarding prizes.
- To support shows and take all necessary steps to advance and protect the interests of fancy rats as exhibition animals and pets.
- To foster and maintain a high standard of excellence in judging and show management.
- To educate and encourage members to adopt and maintain high standards of management and care of fancy rats.
- Recommended Vets List
  The NFRS keeps a register of rat-friendly vets who have been recommended by members. Details are given in Pro-Rat-a, the magazine of the NFRS.

Rat Rescue

The NFRS is not a rescue organisation, and does not have the facilities to act as a clearing house for homeless rats. However, many members take in homeless rats on an individual basis, and most breeders seem to have a number of waifs and strays. Although the NFRS is not able to take in homeless animals, it aims to reduce the need for re-homing by educating pet owners and encouraging them to take responsibility for their rats. Breeders should make sure that they do not sell rats to people who do not take their responsibilities seriously.

National Fancy Rat Society
PO Box 24207
London SE9 5ZF

Rat & Mouse Club of America (RMCA)
Concerned with keeping rats and mice as both pets and exhibition animals, with the emphasis on pet care and rescuing. Publishes a glossy magazine every 2 months with great photos.
13075 Springdale Street #302, Westminster, CA 92683
(714) 892-7523
email: rmca@aol.com
www.rmca.org

American Fancy Rat & Mouse Association (AFRMA)
9230 64th Street, Riverside, CA 92509-5924, USA
email Craig Robbins on craigr@afrma.org
www.afrma.org

Australian Rat Fanciers Society
Phone: (03) 9440-7710 or (03) 9775-9651
Club Address:
PO Box 15
Heidelberg West 3018
http://ausrfs.org.au/index2.html

The Australian Mouse and Rat Information Service,
PO BOX 4248,
Ringwood,
Victoria,
Australia 3134.

http://members.iinet.com.au/~rabbit/ratmouse.htm

Name:	Rat or fancy rat
Latin name:	*Rattus norvegicus*
Order:	Rodents (*Rodentia*)
Sub-order:	Mice and rats (*Muridae*)
Body length:	20 - 27 cm
Tail length:	17 - 23 cm
Weight:	Male: 300 - 580 grams
	Female: 190 - 350 grams
Body temperature:	37.5 - 38.5 degrees
Breathing rate:	85 - 110 per minute
Heart-rate:	300 - 500 per minute
Ambient temperature:	15 - 21, max. 25 degrees
Humidity in %:	45 - 55 % (optimum)
Water intake per day:	20 - 30 ml
Food intake per day:	10 - 15 grams (1 - 1.5 dessert spoons)

Profile

the **Rat**